MERRY CHRISTMAS, HAPPY NEW YEAR

MERRY CHRISTMAS,

DECORATIONS BY ILONKA KARASZ·

HAPPY NEW YEAR

Phyllis McGinley

THE VIKING PRESS · NEW YORK

31927

Contents

Greeting Card for Bibliophiles

A Merry Christmas, Readers, one and all:

Readers of essay or continued story;
You who delight in large print or in small;
You constant readers and you desultory;
Readers in bed; readers in easy chairs
With esoteric tomes upon your laps;
Desk-readers; you who read in middle-air,
Hanging from subway straps;
Readers who munch
A chapter with your lunch
Or only read on evenings when it rains;
Readers on trains;
All you who browse in bookshops, at your clubs,
Or, indolent, in tubs;
Who plump for Plutarch or who love a sequel—
I send you greetings warm and free and equal.

Blessings and little sorrow
On you that lend books; yes, and you that borrow;
All readers, whether stirred
By Aristophanes or comic strip;
You dogged ones that finish every word;
And you that skip;
The margin-scribblers and the question-noters;
Quoters;
Readers of any style,
Young, aging, juvenile.
I wish you well, I wish you very well.

Here's a Noel
To all whom printed pages are not lost on;
Readers in Boise, Boston,
Nantucket, Palo Alto, Kalamazoo—
My love to you and you!

May special angels herald
Jane Austen fans and fans of Scott Fitzgerald;
Book-club subscribers; lovers of Prominent Names;
Addicts of Proust, John Marquand, Henry James;
Dwellers on want ads or financial sections;
And you who gallop off in New Directions;
Inebriate readers, drunkards to the bone,
Forever at your literary tippling,
And you who take a book or leave it alone;
Readers of Kafka (Franz) or Mr. Kipling,
Of Kelland or the Reverend Kierkegaard;
You praisers of the Bard
And you who like your culture by the yard;
All devotees of Agatha Christie, Dickens,
Wodehouse, or Donne;
You who demand a plot that grimly thickens;
You who read Latin poetry for fun
Or like a how-to or a junior-miss-book,
Or even this book.

Until the ultimate Christmas tale is spun,
God bless you, every one.

CHRISTMAS,
CON & PRO

All the Days of Christmas

What shall my true love
Have from me
To pleasure his Christmas
Wealthily?
The partridge has flown
From our pear tree.

Flown with our summers,
Are the swans and the geese.
Milkmaids and drummers
Would leave him little peace.
I've no gold ring
And no turtle dove.
So what can I bring
To my true love?

A coat for the drizzle,
Chosen at the store;
A saw and a chisel
For mending the door;
A pair of red slippers
To slip on his feet;
Three striped neckties;
Something sweet.

He shall have all
I can best afford—
No pipers, piping,
No leaping lord,
But a fine fat hen
For his Christmas board;
Two pretty daughters
(Versed in the role)

To be worn like pinks
In his buttonhole;
And the tree of my heart
With its calling linnet,
My evergreen heart
And the bright bird in it.

Christmas Eve in Our Village

Main Street is gay. Each lamppost glimmers,
  Crowned with a blue, electric star.
The gift tree by our fountain shimmers,
  Superbly tall, if angular
  (Donated by the Men's Bazaar).

With garlands proper to the times
  Our doors are wreathed, our lintels strewn.
From our two steeples sound the chimes,
  Incessant, through the afternoon,
  Only a little out of tune.

Breathless, with boxes hard to handle,
  The grocery drivers come and go.
Madam the Chairman lights a candle
  To introduce our club's tableau.
  The hopeful children pray for snow.

They cluster, mittened, in the park
  To talk of morning, half affrighted,
And early comes the winter dark
  And early are our windows lighted
  To beckon homeward the benighted.

The eggnog's lifted for libation,
  Silent at last the postman's ring,
But on the plaza near the station
  The carolers are caroling.
  "O Little Town!" the carolers sing.

City Christmas

Now is the time when the great urban heart
   More warmly beats, exiling melancholy.
Turkey comes table d'hôte or à la carte.
   Our elevator wears a wreath of holly.

Mendicant Santa Claus in flannel robes
   At every corner contradicts his label,
Alms-asking. We've a tree with colored globes
   In our apartment foyer, on a table.

There is a promise—or a threat—of snow
   Noised by the press. We pull our collars tighter.
And twenty thousand doormen hourly grow
   Politer and politer and politer.

Nicholas, Bishop of Myra's See,
Was holy a saint
As a saint could be;
Saved not a bit
Of his worldly wealth
And loved to commit
Good deeds by stealth.

Was there a poor man,
Wanting a roof?
Nicholas sheltered him weatherproof.
Who lacked a morsel
Had but to ask it
And at his doorsill
Was Nicholas' basket.

O, many a basket did he carry!
Penniless girls
Whom none would marry
Used to discover to their delight,
Into their windows
Tossed at night
(When the moon was old
And the dark was showery),
Bags of gold
Enough for a dowery.

People, I read,
Grew slightly lyrical,
Calling each deed
He did, a miracle.
Told how he calmed the sea for sailors

And rescued children
From awful jailors
Who, drawing lots
For the foul design,
Liked pickling tots
In pickle-brine.

Nicholas, *circa*
Fourth cent. A. D.,
Died in the odor of sanctity.
But fortune changes,
Blessings pass,
And look what's happened to Nicholas.

He who had feared
The world's applause,
Now, with a beard,
Is Santa Claus.
A multiplied elf, he struts and poses,
Ringing up sales
In putty noses;
With Comet and Cupid
His constant partners,
Telling tall tales to kindergart'ners,
His halo fickle as
Wind and wave.

While dizzily Nicholas
Spins in his grave.

Dear Madam: We Know

You Will Want to Contribute...

Christmas is coming,
The geese are getting fat.
Please to put a penny in an old man's hat.
If you haven't got a penny, a ha' penny will do.
If you haven't got a ha' penny, God help you!

Please to put a nickel,
    Please to put a dime.
How petitions trickle
    In at Christmas time!
Come and Save a Scholar.
    Bring the heathen hope.
Just enclose a dollar
    Within the envelope.
Send along a tenner,
    Anyhow a five,
And let the Friends of Poetry inaugurate their drive.

Share your weekly ration
    With miners up in Nome.
Give a small donation
    To build a Starlings' Home.
Please to send a shillin'
    For lawyers in the lurch.
Drop a pretty bill in
    The offering at church.
Remember all the orphans,
    Recall the boys at camps,
And decorate your letters with illuminated stamps.

The Common Colds Committee
    Implores you to assist.
They're canvassing the city,
    They've got you on their list.
Demonstrate your mettle
    For half a hundred causes.
Fill the yawning kettle
    Of the corner Santa Clauses.
Give for holy Charity
    Wherever she appears.
And don't forget the Firemen and the Southern Mountaineers.

Christmas is coming,
The mail is getting fat.
Please to put a penny in every proffered hat.
If you haven't got a penny, a ha' pence let it be.
If you haven't got a ha' pence left, you're just like me.

What Every Woman Knows

When little boys are able
   To comprehend the flaws
In their December fable
   And part with Santa Claus,
Although I do not think they grieve,
How burningly they disbelieve!

They cannot wait, they cannot rest
For knowledge nibbling at the breast.
They cannot rest, they cannot wait
To set conniving parents straight.

Branding that comrade as a dunce
Who trusts the saint they trusted once,
With rude guffaw and facial spasm
They publish their iconoclasm,
And find particularly shocking
The thought of hanging up a stocking.

But little girls (no blinder
   When faced by mortal fact)
Are cleverer and kinder
   And brimming full of tact.
The knowingness of little girls
Is hidden underneath their curls.

Obligingly, since parents fancy
The season's tinsel necromancy,
They take some pains to make pretense
Of duped and eager innocence.

Agnostics born but Bernhardts bred,
They hang the stocking by the bed,
Make plans, and pleasure their begetters
By writing Santa lengthy letters,
Only too well aware the fruit
Is shinier plunder, richer loot.

For little boys are rancorous
  When robbed of any myth,
And spiteful and cantankerous
  To all their kin and kith.
But little girls can draw conclusions
And profit from their lost illusions.

Whatever's got into Christmas?
  It happens so often now.
When I was six or a little bit more,
Though we popped the corn and we dressed the door,
  Though we trimmed the spicy bough,
This festival morn, this midnight clear,
They only enveloped us once a year.
While now, as the world and I grow older,
Christmas keeps peering round my shoulder.

When I was seven or maybe eight,
The year crawled past like a snowbound freight.
Centuries yawned, I well remember,
Between December and next December.

But now I'm a grown-up more or less,
The Yule pulls in like a fast express.
St. Nick's forever cutting a caper.
I'm always knee-deep in tissue paper.

Wherever I look, whenever I listen,
The joy-bells ring and the gift-cards glisten.
While last year's candles are still aglow,
I'm kissed under this year's mistletoe.

Noel has bound me in chains and fetters.
Just as I'm starting my thank-you letters,
The carols begin and a crooner hummeth
And lo! the sedulous mailman cometh.

Ah, twelve were the days of Christmas,
    But that was a long time back.
For now so swiftly do they arrive
It's more like three hundred sixty-five
    In my personal almanac.
And somehow my *joie de vivre* gets drowsy
With everything always so Wenceslausy.
I might love Christmas
A bushel and a peck,
Would it only stop breathing down my neck.

Enigma for Christmas Shoppers

It is a strange, miraculous thing
   About department stores,
How elevators upward wing
   By twos and threes and fours,

How pale lights gleam, how cables run
   All day without an end,
Yet how reluctant, one by one,
   The homing cars descend.

They soar to Furniture, or higher,
   They speed to Gowns and Gifts,
But when the bought weighs down the buyer,
   Late, late, return the lifts.

Newton himself, beneath his tree,
   Would ponder this and frown;
How what goes up so frequently
   So seldom, here, comes down.

Office Party

This holy night in open forum
   Miss McIntosh, who handles Files,
Has lost one shoe and her decorum.
   Stately, the frozen chairman smiles

On Media, desperately vocal.
   Credit, though they have lost their hopes
Of edging toward an early Local,
   Finger their bonus envelopes.

The glassy boys, the bursting girls
   Of Copy, start a Conga clatter
To a swung carol. Limply curls
   The final sandwich on the platter

Till hark! a herald Messenger
   (Room 414) lifts loudly up
His quavering tenor. Salesmen stir
   Libation for his Lily cup.

"Noel," he pipes, "Noel, Noel."
   Some wag beats tempo with a ruler.
And the plump blonde from Personnel
   Collapses by the water cooler.

Bootless Speculations

ON THE IMPRACTICALITY OF FULFILLING
A DAUGHTER'S CHRISTMAS REQUEST FOR SILVER SHOES

One fact eccentric I often muse on:
Girls of sixteen won't keep their shoes on.

Girls, at sixteen, for all our strictures,
Are proper as Puritans,
Pretty as pictures.
With waists cinched tightly,
Wearing ponytails,
They move more lightly
Than a ship with sails,
Than roses shaking
The summer dews off—
But why must they always be taking their shoes off?

Girls of sixteen
Have rows and rows
Of fanciful, lean
Capezios.
Helter-skelter,
To point of scandal,

24

Their closets shelter
Slipper and sandal,
Glass shoes, gilt shoes,
Shoes with baubles on,
Three-inch-stilt shoes
That everyone wobbles on,
Shoes gone risible,
Shoes for sport,
Shoes without visible
Means of support.
Each maidenly foot is a clad-with-care foot,
But how do they go?
Why, chiefly barefoot.

They never enter
Their entrance halls
But front and center
The footwear falls:
Pumps under sofas;
Brogues on the stairs;
Loathsome loafers
Beneath wing chairs;
Shoes on the landing,
Lost in flight;
On porches standing
Overnight,
While, legs a-taper,
Combing their curls,
Blithely caper
The discalced girls.
Shoeless they chatter their gossip windy
Or barefoot at parties
Dance the Lindy.

For girls at sixteen have depths unsounded.
Of sugar and spice
Are they compounded;
Sweetly their powers
Shame doubting Thomases;
They keep late hours
But keep their promises;
They keep cool heads
For the course they cruise on.
So why in the world can't they keep their shoes on?

Oh, Come, Little Children

What man of ignorance undefiled
First praised the prattle of a child
Or called its stumbling accents gentle?
He was a fraud, and sentimental,
Some lout whose premise I deplore—
A hermit or a bachelor.

No babes of my acquaintance speak
In syllables below a shriek.
This golden boy, this dimpled bouncer,
Studies to be a train announcer.
That rose-lipped girl with tresses flaxen
Outdoes, by any odds, the klaxon.
In the bright lexicon of lispers
There's no such word as "whispers."

Calliopes chant soft and formally
Compared to tots conversing normally,
While in the wails of urchins crossed,
The riveter's refrain is lost.
Articulate, they come and go,
But never pianissimo.

I'll wager—coming to the heart of this—
That fellow mentioned at the start of this
Had no experience, even cursory,
With pretty babblings from a nursery,
Or his fine lines had died aborning
At six o'clock some Christmas morning.

Lady Selecting Her Christmas Cards

Fastidiously, with gloved and careful fingers,
    Through the marked samples she pursues her search.
Which shall it be: the snowscape's wintry languors
    Complete with church,

An urban skyline, children sweetly pretty
    Sledding downhill, the chaste, ubiquitous wreath,
Schooner or candle or the simple Scottie
    With verse underneath?

Perhaps it might be better to emblazon
    With words alone the stiff, punctilious square.
(Oh, not Victorian, certainly. This season
    One meets it everywhere.)

She has a duty proper to the weather—
    A Birth she must announce, a rumor to spread,
Wherefore the very spheres once sang together
    And a star shone overhead.

Here are the Tidings which the shepherds panted
    One to another, kneeling by their flocks.
And they will bear her name (engraved, not printed),
    Twelve-fifty for the box.

Open Letter to Santa Claus

Dear Kringle or Whomever This Concerns:

Before a Yule log burns
Or the first fir tree teeters on its stand,
I take my pen in hand
(Take, anyhow, a pencil in my fist)
And write this little list
Of festal boons, ingenious but sterile,
You bring me at your peril.
Here is fair warning
Of what I do not want on Christmas morning.

For instance, lamps. Fetch me no lamps of pottery,
No lamps beloved of gift shops and of brides,
No tasseled lamps from rummage sale or lottery,
None planted with ivy sprouting at the sides,
Or fashioned out of canister or churn
Discarded (rightly) by one's Grams and Gramps,
No lamps Chinese or period or Moderne.
No lamps.

Also, I would prefer
No bath towels coyly lettered HIM and HER;
No matches, monogrammed; no cocktail glasses
(Planned for the rumpus rooms of those who've got'm)
With naughty silhouettes of Gallic lasses
Painted upon the bottom;
No dubious napery
Personalized and papery;
No hand-blocked scarves designed to wrap the head in;
No bedroom slippers

That fools as well as angels fear to tread in;
No gloves with zippers.

Likewise, I beg you, curb
Your passion for the culinary herb,
Which, though no doubt divine to flavor stew with,
I don't know what to do with.

Avoid the bath salts and the cloisonné;
The diary refillable as to leaf;
The ash—or any other kind of—tray;
The colored handkerchief;
The deck of cards with pictures of Mount Shasta on;
The pad to score Canasta on.
(In fact, best star this item with an asterisk:
I am a bad Canasta risk.)
Ah, call it treason,
But spare me, sir, such horrors of the season.
My wants are easy, small, and quickly spoken.
Leave for me
As seal of faith, as merely holiday token,
Some minor bauble underneath the tree:
Perhaps a gilt-edged bond,
Some modest pearl or simple diamond,
Or—let me think—
Something as casual as a basic mink
To shelter me from winter's chills and damps
When blizzards threaten and the blood runs thinly.

But, sir, no lamps!

Yours faithfully,
PHYLLIS McGINLEY

The Holy City

(Verses written during the unquiet in Israel, when Sabbath bugles were replaced by bells and town criers so they could not be confused with air-raid sirens.)

In Palestine, in Palestine,
The mantled shepherds keep
Their watches still
On every hill
    Where flocks, unsheltered, sleep.

And people walk with living fear
    Lest, singing while it fell,
Should shine upon some midnight clear
    The star that is a shell.

Loud are the bells in Palestine
    Where there's a sentry stationed,
And still the oil and still the wine
    Are blessed before they're rationed,

And criers chant the Sabbath for
    The faithful and the stranger.
But now the bugles blow no more
    Except the song of danger.

Lower your gates, Jerusalem.
Make mute the sacred horn
While dark comes down
Upon that town
    Wherein the Light was born.

How the Beasts Keep Christmas

At midnight's stroke,
In barn, in stall,
Kneel all
The dumb folk.

Meekly bow
In reverence, then,
The silly hen,
The horned cow,

For a breath's space.
And ass and ox
Makes, each, his box
A kneeling place.

Even the dark
Forest peoples
Hear the steeple's
"Hark! Hark!"

And glory wheels
Through den and lair.
Beside the hare
Fox kneels,

Till all on earth
Of fur or feather
Praise together
Christ's birth,

The when or why
Can none recall,
Yet kneel all.
And kneel I.

The Ballad of Befana

AN EPIPHANY LEGEND

Befana the Housewife, scrubbing her pane,
Saw three old sages ride down the lane,
Saw three gray travelers pass her door—
Gaspar, Balthazar, Melchior.

"Where journey you, sirs?" she asked of them.
Balthazar answered, "To Bethlehem,

For we have news of a marvelous thing.
Born in a stable is Christ the King."

"Give Him my welcome!"
Then Gaspar smiled,
"Come with us, mistress, to greet the Child."

"Oh, happily, happily would I fare,
Were my dusting through and I'd polished the stair."

Old Melchior leaned on his saddle horn.
"Then send but a gift to the small Newborn."

"Oh, gladly, gladly I'd send Him one,
Were the hearthstone swept and my weaving done.

"As soon as ever I've baked my bread,
I'll fetch Him a pillow for His head,
And a coverlet too," Befana said.

"When the rooms are aired and the linen dry,
I'll look at the Babe."
But the Three rode by.

She worked for a day and a night and a day,
Then, gifts in her hands, took up her way.
But she never could find where the Christ Child lay.

And still she wanders at Christmastide,
Houseless, whose house was all her pride,

Whose heart was tardy, whose gifts were late;
Wanders, and knocks at every gate,
Crying, "Good people, the bells begin!
Put off your toiling and let love in."

Twelfth Night

Down from the window take the withered holly.
Feed the torn tissue to the literal blaze.
Now, now at last are come the melancholy
Anticlimatic days.

Here in the light of morning, hard, unvarnished,
Let us with haste dismantle the tired tree
Of ornaments, a trifle chipped and tarnished,
Pretend we do not see

How all the rooms seem shabbier and meaner
And the tired house a little less than snug.
Fold up the tinsel. Run the vacuum cleaner
Over the littered rug.

Nothing is left. The postman passes by, now,
Bearing no gifts, no kind or seasonal word.
The icebox yields no wing, no nibbled thigh, now,
From any holiday bird.

Sharp in the streets the north wind plagues its betters
While Christmas snow to-gutters is consigned.
Nothing remains except the thank-you letters,
Most tedious to the mind,

And the gilt gadget (duplicated) which is
Marked for exchange at Abercrombie-Fitch's.

NEW YEAR & NO RESOLUTIONS

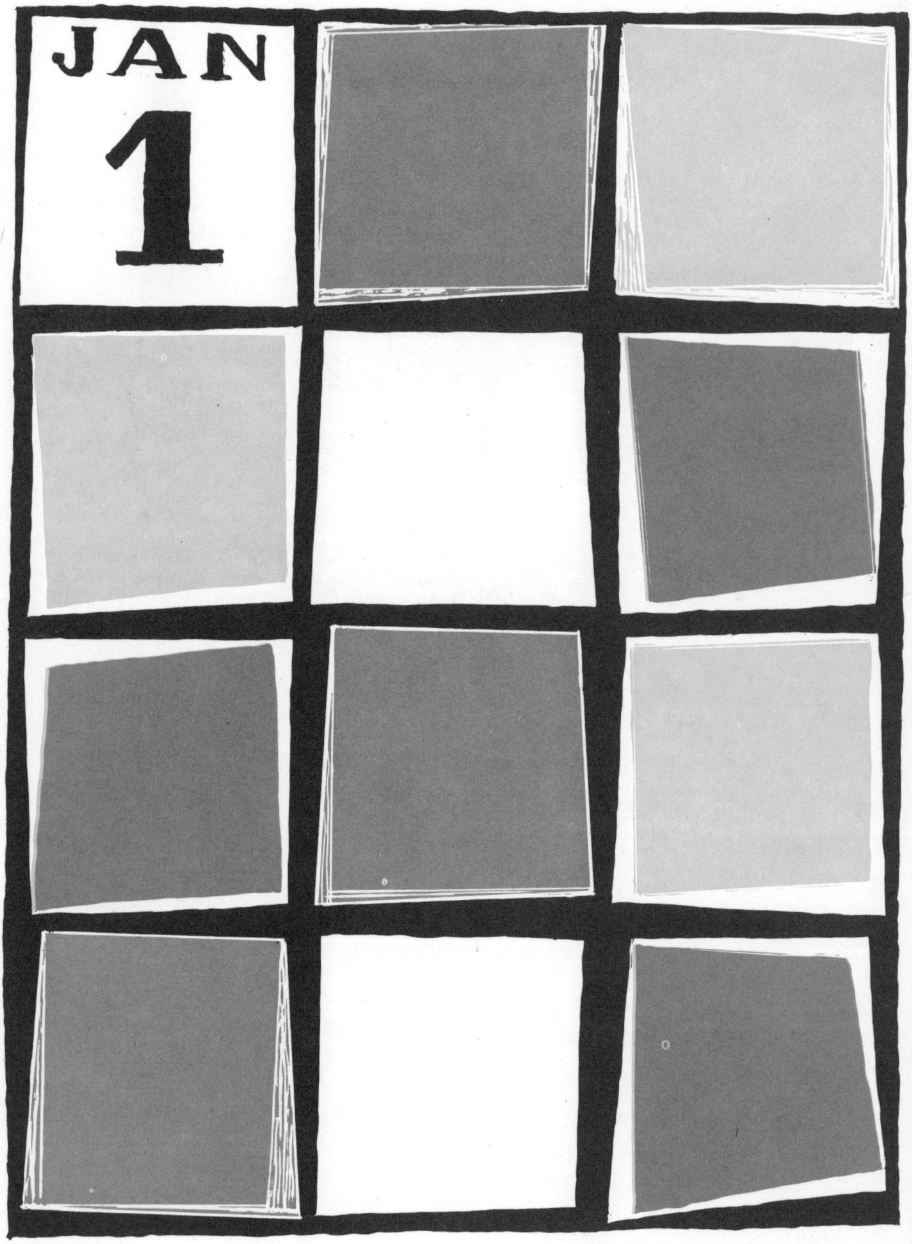
JAN
1

There's this to be said for making New Year's resolutions: it is good clean sport—one that limbers the imagination, flexes the muscles of the character, and adds a kind of rough-and-tumble zest to those dreary weeks immediately following the winter holidays.

But like most forms of exercise, it should be indulged in with moderation—particularly as one reaches the wiser, or declining, years. After all, wrestling with temptation can be as exhausting as any other sort of athletics and can result in a variety of wounds and traumas—fractured egos, tempers thrown out of joint, lumbagos of the spirit. I'm not sure anyone over forty should *make* a resolution.

Particularly not on the first of January. Of all the bleak, dark, unthinkable times to write out a prescription for improvement, January is the bleakest and darkest and most inauspicious. The high fever of Christmas has only just burned itself out; on its heels comes the New Year's relapse. And it is in this invalid condition that across the length and breadth of the land people decide to remold their behavior or their careers or their figures closer to some Technicolor ideal. Is it any wonder they are foredoomed to failure? The very month conspires against them, adding the spites and angers of storm, bursting steampipes, and delinquent progeny to the misery of blessings withdrawn. Nothing can possibly get a decent start in the depths of winter except a nasty, nagging cold.

And yet the temptation to make resolutions is something I've not been able to overcome. "This year," I tell myself, "no promises!" But let one wild bell ring out, let me get halfway through a chorus of "Auld Lang Syne," and I find myself vowing that, come tomorrow, I'll begin my program of bending from the waist fifty times, night and morning, or answering all my letters the day they reach me. And it's sometimes as late as February before I've won the struggle against my Better Self. It takes strength of character not to give in to good resolves.

But one must fight off the impulse. For resolutions made under a sprig of fading mistletoe are generally the wrong type for January. I can imagine someone's vowing to cross a desert or lead a crusade or build a rocket to the moon and managing it triumphantly. Those are active aspirations and they'd keep one's mind off the weather. But in a season that cries out for small solaces, we keep on giving up things.

We promise to deprive ourselves of the trivial comforts that may be all that stand between us and frenzy. Coffee, for instance, or that martini before dinner. Strong with the spurious courage lent by a yet unspotted calendar, we abstain from cigarettes. Are we chatterers by nature, loving the neighborly tidbit on the tongue? Then we swear to forego gossip and be succinct on the telephone.

Or else we vow to shun the second helping of chicken with dumplings and that cream puff for dessert, to live horribly on cottage cheese and pineapple for our waistline's sake. Somehow we persuade ourselves that, however dismal the soggy landscape and the winter afternoons, cutting down on our pleasures will bring the roses to our cheeks and the bonus to our pay envelopes.

44

Or else we acquire a compulsion toward Culture. We cancel our reserve copy of *Murder at the Glove Counter* and resolve to give *War and Peace* another chance. Some of us so far lose our heads as to make resolutions about how we'll treat our children. We'll give up scolding them, we assert; we'll try to make friends with them instead and invite their confidences.

Folly, folly, all folly! Those promises might stand a chance of being kept in June, say, with the spirits burgeoning along with roses and summer barbecues. In spring, when the year really begins. But in winter, no.

My plan calls for giving up no luxurious bad habit. I shall try only to savor each with more contentment. That plumpness around the midriff may be insurance against nagging at the dinner table. Fortified by that extra cup of coffee in the morning, I can kiss my husband off to work serenely. And I shan't mind which television station he insists on watching, so long as I am not going cigaretteless through the evening. Besides, how do I know—since doctors still debate the issue —that science will not some day decree there is a necessary vitamin in tobacco or something especially nutritious in caffeine? Wouldn't I feel silly then, having spent all that anguish of mind in doing without them?

Up, then, with the guilty cup, the avoirdupois, the cigarette! My sincerest efforts shall lie in taking more pains with the percolator and improving my recipe for crêpes suzette.

The same goes for the other indulgences. Give up gossip? Why, it's the very stuff that talk is made on. What is any conversation worth that doesn't include it? Even the dictionary bears me out. Its lovely derivation is "God-sib" and it refers to a godparent who, it is to be supposed, once brought into the welcoming house his own brand of ineffable tattle. Gossip isn't scandal and it's not merely malicious. It's chatter about the human race by lovers of the same. Gossip is the tool of the poet, the shoptalk of the scientist, the consolation of housewife, wit, tycoon, and intellectual. It begins in the nursery and ends when speech is past. Who am I to fly in the face of nature? Besides, consider the mischief-makers of the universe. They are not the gossips, but the reformers and the puritans and the witch-burners and the keepers of resolutions. They *do* things. They drop bombs and search out heretics. Untobaccoed, coffeeless, and without humor, they start the wars or set the juggernauts rolling. But the gossips, happily employed with discussing Mrs. Lilywhite's peculiar behavior at the club dance or whether young Jones is serious about that girl in Tallahassee, are having too pleasant a time to upset the status quo.

Perhaps the word has fallen into disrepute because it's so often linked with "idle." But what, I ask myself again, is wrong with a bit of idleness? To waste a little time, to stop one's customary busyness and look around at the world in which one holds so brief a tenure—these are not unadmirable occupations. The Devil finds work for idle hands, says the old saw. But you notice that it's the *work* that's castigated, not the contemplation. When I recall all the sunsets I've missed, all the glimpses of apple trees and feathery snowstorms and faces of passers-by, lost because some commonplace task was too absorbing to put off, I've sworn to be more idle rather than less in the new year. Let meals be half an hour late or a table go undusted. When there's sun, I'll sit in it. When the spring rain is particularly appealing, I'll walk in it. I'll put second-class mail straight in the wastebasket without reading it and stop scouring corners except on days when nothing worthier calls. If I find it rewarding to sit down in the middle of a cluttered morning and read a book, I'll do that too.

But I shan't make any promises about the importance of my reading. At my time of life—at anybody's time of life— reading shouldn't be for duty only, even if duty consists merely in keeping up with the best sellers. Otherwise one of the great consolations of existence grows tarnished. I'll read as I please—a spot of science fiction, a taste of Jane Austen. Mark Twain and Keats and Agatha Christie shall sit cheek by jowl on my night table. And I'll make it a point of honor to finish no book I'm not enjoying, also to skip as much and as often as I like. If I want to peek to see how a novel comes out, I'll feel perfectly justified. I'll go to Plato when I'm in the mood and the newest thriller when I'm not. For again, the little vices bring relaxation; and a bit of trash now and then is good for the severest reader. It provides that necessary roughage in the literary diet.

As to improving my footing with the children, I'll shun *that* trap altogether. The flaw in too many "child-parent rela- tionships" (to quote the current jargon) is the amount of fussing about it that mothers and fathers do. Children from ten to twenty don't *want* to be understood. Their whole ambition is to feel strange and alien and misinterpreted so that they can live austerely in some stone tower of adoles- cence, their privacies unviolated. There's nothing they resent more than their elders' feebleminded attempts to make friends. To them that's not comradeship, but prying. Author- ity they will accept. It's something to complain about and to rest against. But their confidences come only when they're not applied for.

And while I'm about it, let me add a word of counsel. Parents ought to thank providence when their children *don't* constantly confide in them. Hearing the confidences of the young can be as wearying as it is flattering and is chiefly required at eleven-fifty-five on Sunday night just when one is most comfortably in bed, set about with pillows, and eager to find out who killed the blonde in Lord Stanhope's library.

To ignore my progeny, then; to skimp the housework, to gossip over cups of coffee and cigarettes, to let the pounds and the great books fall where they will; are those reputable goals for a human being and a citizen? I think perhaps they are. At least in January. They are the lesser lapses I shall cultivate to combat the larger ones of greed, ambition, faultfinding, spite, and envy. If I let myself have my head on the small vices, maybe I'll have time to encourage the small benignities like admiring my husband's jokes or my friend's hairdo. I'll keep blithe enough to give a compliment when it's needed, listen to Bach done to "Lute, Harpsichord, and Consort of Viols," and see the winter through without an ulcer.

If I ever feel myself genuinely on fire for a fling at heroism or sainthood, I'll choose a different time. There'll be sun beaming away like a rich uncle and dogwood budding and the earth spicy with flowers and fertilizer.

But that will be some lacquered day in April, at the genuine beginning of the year.

Merry Christmas - Happy New Year

to Mary with love

from Kathryn and Reid

De la amiga.
Estados Unidos   12/20/58